A
Politician's
Bucket List
Book

Peter Churchill

Preface

A life of a politician is never easy when it comes to running the country that you are in politics in is it?

Hassle after hassle to get things right when you can, even if you are not in the party that is in power.

This Bucket list book is something for a politician to write down the ideas and plans to get things right in life while in the job of a politician.

I have been able to achieve dreams myself by doing it the way that this book shows.

Let's get started on achieving your goals.

Peter Churchill

My Bucket Wish List 1.

Wish:

Start Date -
End Date -

Goals to reach my wish/project :

1.

2.

3.

4.

5.

6.

7.

My Bucket Wish List 2.

Wish:

Start Date -
End Date -

Goals to reach my wish/project :

1.

2.

3.

4.

5.

6.

7.

My Bucket Wish List 3.

Wish:

Start Date -
End Date -

Goals to reach my wish/project :

1.

2.

3.

4.

5.

6.

7.

My Bucket Wish List 4.

Wish:

Start Date -
End Date -

Goals to reach my wish/project :

1.

2.

3.

4.

5.

6.

7.

My Bucket Wish List 5.

Wish:

Start Date -
End Date -

Goals to reach my wish/project :

1.

2.

3.

4.

5.

6.

7.

My Bucket Wish List 6.

Wish:

Start Date -
End Date -

Goals to reach my wish/project :

1.

2.

3.

4.

5.

6.

7.

My Bucket Wish List 7.

Wish:

Start Date -
End Date -

Goals to reach my wish/project :

1.

2.

3.

4.

5.

6.

7.

My Bucket Wish List 8.

Wish:

Start Date -
End Date -

Goals to reach my wish/project :

1.

2.

3.

4.

5.

6.

7.

My Bucket Wish List 9.

Wish:

Start Date -
End Date -

Goals to reach my wish/project :

1.

2.

3.

4.

5.

6.

7.

My Bucket Wish List 10.

Wish:

Start Date -
End Date -

Goals to reach my wish/project :

1.

2.

3.

4.

5.

6.

7.

My Bucket Wish List 11.

Wish:

Start Date -
End Date -

Goals to reach my wish/project :

1.

2.

3.

4.

5.

6.

7.

My Bucket Wish List 12.

Wish:

Start Date -
End Date -

Goals to reach my wish/project :

1.

2.

3.

4.

5.

6.

7.

My Bucket Wish List 13.

Wish:

Start Date -
End Date -

Goals to reach my wish/project :

1.

2.

3.

4.

5.

6.

7.

My Bucket Wish List 14.

Wish:

Start Date -
End Date -

Goals to reach my wish/project :

1.

2.

3.

4.

5.

6.

7.

My Bucket Wish List 15.

Wish:

Start Date -
End Date -

Goals to reach my wish/project :

1.

2.

3.

4.

5.

6.

7.

My Bucket Wish List 16.

Wish:

Start Date -
End Date -

Goals to reach my wish/project :

1.

2.

3.

4.

5.

6.

7.

My Bucket Wish List 17.

Wish:

Start Date -
End Date -

Goals to reach my wish/project :

1.

2.

3.

4.

5.

6.

7.

My Bucket Wish List 18.

Wish:

Start Date -
End Date -

Goals to reach my wish/project :

1.

2.

3.

4.

5.

6.

7.

My Bucket Wish List 19.

Wish:

Start Date -
End Date -

Goals to reach my wish/project :

1.

2.

3.

4.

5.

6.

7.

My Bucket Wish List 20.

Wish:

Start Date -
End Date -

Goals to reach my wish/project :

1.

2.

3.

4.

5.

6.

7.

My Bucket Wish List 21.

Wish:

Start Date -
End Date -

Goals to reach my wish/project :

1.

2.

3.

4.

5.

6.

7.

My Bucket Wish List 22.

Wish:

Start Date -
End Date -

Goals to reach my wish/project :

1.

2.

3.

4.

5.

6.

7.

My Bucket Wish List 23.

Wish:

Start Date -
End Date -

Goals to reach my wish/project :

1.

2.

3.

4.

5.

6.

7.

My Bucket Wish List 24.

Wish:

Start Date -
End Date -

Goals to reach my wish/project :

1.

2.

3.

4.

5.

6.

7.

My Bucket Wish List 25.

Wish:

Start Date -
End Date -

Goals to reach my wish/project :

1.

2.

3.

4.

5.

6.

7.

My Bucket Wish List 26.

Wish:

Start Date -
End Date -

Goals to reach my wish/project :

1.

2.

3.

4.

5.

6.

7.

My Bucket Wish List 27.

Wish:

Start Date -
End Date -

Goals to reach my wish/project :

1.

2.

3.

4.

5.

6.

7.

My Bucket Wish List 28.

Wish:

Start Date -
End Date -

Goals to reach my wish/project :

1.

2.

3.

4.

5.

6.

7.

My Bucket Wish List 29.

Wish:

Start Date -
End Date -

Goals to reach my wish/project :

1.

2.

3.

4.

5.

6.

7.

My Bucket Wish List 30.

Wish:

Start Date -
End Date -

Goals to reach my wish/project :

1.

2.

3.

4.

5.

6.

7.

My Bucket Wish List 31.

Wish:

Start Date -
End Date -

Goals to reach my wish/project :

1.

2.

3.

4.

5.

6.

7.

My Bucket Wish List 32.

Wish:

Start Date -
End Date -

Goals to reach my wish/project :

1.

2.

3.

4.

5.

6.

7.

My Bucket Wish List 33.

Wish:

Start Date -
End Date -

Goals to reach my wish/project :

1.

2.

3.

4.

5.

6.

7.

My Bucket Wish List 34.

Wish:

Start Date -
End Date -

Goals to reach my wish/project :

1.

2.

3.

4.

5.

6.

7.

My Bucket Wish List 35.

Wish:

Start Date -
End Date -

Goals to reach my wish/project :

1.

2.

3.

4.

5.

6.

7.

My Bucket Wish List 36.

Wish:

Start Date -
End Date -

Goals to reach my wish/project :

1.

2.

3.

4.

5.

6.

7.

My Bucket Wish List 37.

Wish:

Start Date -
End Date -

Goals to reach my wish/project :

1.

2.

3.

4.

5.

6.

7.

My Bucket Wish List 38.

Wish:

Start Date -
End Date -

Goals to reach my wish/project :

1.

2.

3.

4.

5.

6.

7.

My Bucket Wish List 39.

Wish:

Start Date -
End Date -

Goals to reach my wish/project :

1.

2.

3.

4.

5.

6.

7.

My Bucket Wish List 40.

Wish:

Start Date -
End Date -

Goals to reach my wish/project :

1.

2.

3.

4.

5.

6.

7.

My Bucket Wish List 41.

Wish:

Start Date -
End Date -

Goals to reach my wish/project :

1.

2.

3.

4.

5.

6.

7.

My Bucket Wish List 42.

Wish:

Start Date -
End Date -

Goals to reach my wish/project :

1.

2.

3.

4.

5.

6.

7.

My Bucket Wish List 43.

Wish:

Start Date -
End Date -

Goals to reach my wish/project :

1.

2.

3.

4.

5.

6.

7.

My Bucket Wish List 44.

Wish:

Start Date -
End Date -

Goals to reach my wish/project :

1.

2.

3.

4.

5.

6.

7.

My Bucket Wish List 45.

Wish:

Start Date -
End Date -

Goals to reach my wish/project :

1.

2.

3.

4.

5.

6.

7.

My Bucket Wish List 46.

Wish:

Start Date -
End Date -

Goals to reach my wish/project :

1.

2.

3.

4.

5.

6.

7.

My Bucket Wish List 47.

Wish:

Start Date -
End Date -

Goals to reach my wish/project :

1.

2.

3.

4.

5.

6.

7.

My Bucket Wish List 48.

Wish:

Start Date -
End Date -

Goals to reach my wish/project :

1.

2.

3.

4.

5.

6.

7.

My Bucket Wish List 49.

Wish:

Start Date -
End Date -

Goals to reach my wish/project :

1.

2.

3.

4.

5.

6.

7.

My Bucket Wish List 50.

Wish:

Start Date -
End Date -

Goals to reach my wish/project :

1.

2.

3.

4.

5.

6.

7.

My Bucket Wish List 51.

Wish:

Start Date -
End Date -

Goals to reach my wish/project :

1.

2.

3.

4.

5.

6.

7.

My Bucket Wish List 52.

Wish:

Start Date -
End Date -

Goals to reach my wish/project :

1.

2.

3.

4.

5.

6.

7.

My Bucket Wish List 53.

Wish:

Start Date -
End Date -

Goals to reach my wish/project :

1.

2.

3.

4.

5.

6.

7.

My Bucket Wish List 54.

Wish:

Start Date -
End Date -

Goals to reach my wish/project :

1.

2.

3.

4.

5.

6.

7.

My Bucket Wish List 55.

Wish:

Start Date -
End Date -

Goals to reach my wish/project :

1.

2.

3.

4.

5.

6.

7.

My Bucket Wish List 56.

Wish:

Start Date -
End Date -

Goals to reach my wish/project :

1.

2.

3.

4.

5.

6.

7.

My Bucket Wish List 57.

Wish:

Start Date -
End Date -

Goals to reach my wish/project :

1.

2.

3.

4.

5.

6.

7.

My Bucket Wish List 58.

Wish:

Start Date -
End Date -

Goals to reach my wish/project :

1.

2.

3.

4.

5.

6.

7.

My Bucket Wish List 59.

Wish:

Start Date -
End Date -

Goals to reach my wish/project :

1.

2.

3.

4.

5.

6.

7.

My Bucket Wish List 60.

Wish:

Start Date -
End Date -

Goals to reach my wish/project :

1.

2.

3.

4.

5.

6.

7.

My Bucket Wish List 61.

Wish:

Start Date -
End Date -

Goals to reach my wish/project :

1.

2.

3.

4.

5.

6.

7.

My Bucket Wish List 62.

Wish:

Start Date -
End Date -

Goals to reach my wish/project :

1.

2.

3.

4.

5.

6.

7.

My Bucket Wish List 63.

Wish:

Start Date -
End Date -

Goals to reach my wish/project :

1.

2.

3.

4.

5.

6.

7.

My Bucket Wish List 64.

Wish:

Start Date -
End Date -

Goals to reach my wish/project :

1.

2.

3.

4.

5.

6.

7.

My Bucket Wish List 65.

Wish:

Start Date -
End Date -

Goals to reach my wish/project :

1.

2.

3.

4.

5.

6.

7.

My Bucket Wish List 66.

Wish:

Start Date -
End Date -

Goals to reach my wish/project :

1.

2.

3.

4.

5.

6.

7.

My Bucket Wish List 67.

Wish:

Start Date -
End Date -

Goals to reach my wish/project :

1.

2.

3.

4.

5.

6.

7.

My Bucket Wish List 68.

Wish:

Start Date -
End Date -

Goals to reach my wish/project :

1.

2.

3.

4.

5.

6.

7.

My Bucket Wish List 69.

Wish:

Start Date -
End Date -

Goals to reach my wish/project :

1.

2.

3.

4.

5.

6.

7.

My Bucket Wish List 70.

Wish:

Start Date -
End Date -

Goals to reach my wish/project :

1.

2.

3.

4.

5.

6.

7.

My Bucket Wish List 71.

Wish:

Start Date -
End Date -

Goals to reach my wish/project :

1.

2.

3.

4.

5.

6.

7.

My Bucket Wish List 72.

Wish:

Start Date -
End Date -

Goals to reach my wish/project :

1.

2.

3.

4.

5.

6.

7.

My Bucket Wish List 73.

Wish:

Start Date -
End Date -

Goals to reach my wish/project :

1.

2.

3.

4.

5.

6.

7.

My Bucket Wish List 74.

Wish:

Start Date -
End Date -

Goals to reach my wish/project :

1.

2.

3.

4.

5.

6.

7.

My Bucket Wish List 75.

Wish:

Start Date -
End Date -

Goals to reach my wish/project :

1.

2.

3.

4.

5.

6.

7.

My Bucket Wish List 76.

Wish:

Start Date -
End Date -

Goals to reach my wish/project :

1.

2.

3.

4.

5.

6.

7.

My Bucket Wish List 77.

Wish:

Start Date -
End Date -

Goals to reach my wish/project :

1.

2.

3.

4.

5.

6.

7.

My Bucket Wish List 78.

Wish:

Start Date -
End Date -

Goals to reach my wish/project :

1.

2.

3.

4.

5.

6.

7.

My Bucket Wish List 79.

Wish:

Start Date -
End Date -

Goals to reach my wish/project :

1.

2.

3.

4.

5.

6.

7.

My Bucket Wish List 80.

Wish:

Start Date -
End Date -

Goals to reach my wish/project :

1.

2.

3.

4.

5.

6.

7.

My Bucket Wish List 81.

Wish:

Start Date -
End Date -

Goals to reach my wish/project :

1.

2.

3.

4.

5.

6.

7.

My Bucket Wish List 82.

Wish:

Start Date -
End Date -

Goals to reach my wish/project :

1.

2.

3.

4.

5.

6.

7.

My Bucket Wish List 83.

Wish:

Start Date -
End Date -

Goals to reach my wish/project :

1.

2.

3.

4.

5.

6.

7.

My Bucket Wish List 84.

Wish:

Start Date -
End Date -

Goals to reach my wish/project :

1.

2.

3.

4.

5.

6.

7.

My Bucket Wish List 85.

Wish:

Start Date -
End Date -

Goals to reach my wish/project :

1.

2.

3.

4.

5.

6.

7.

My Bucket Wish List 86.

Wish:

Start Date -
End Date -

Goals to reach my wish/project :

1.

2.

3.

4.

5.

6.

7.

My Bucket Wish List 87.

Wish:

Start Date -
End Date -

Goals to reach my wish/project :

1.

2.

3.

4.

5.

6.

7.

My Bucket Wish List 88.

Wish:

Start Date -
End Date -

Goals to reach my wish/project :

1.

2.

3.

4.

5.

6.

7.

My Bucket Wish List 89.

Wish:

Start Date -
End Date -

Goals to reach my wish/project :

1.

2.

3.

4.

5.

6.

7.

My Bucket Wish List 90.

Wish:

Start Date -
End Date -

Goals to reach my wish/project :

1.

2.

3.

4.

5.

6.

7.

My Bucket Wish List 91.

Wish:

Start Date -
End Date -

Goals to reach my wish/project :

1.

2.

3.

4.

5.

6.

7.

My Bucket Wish List 92.

Wish:

Start Date -
End Date -

Goals to reach my wish/project :

1.

2.

3.

4.

5.

6.

7.

My Bucket Wish List 93.

Wish:

Start Date -
End Date -

Goals to reach my wish/project :

1.

2.

3.

4.

5.

6.

7.

My Bucket Wish List 94.

Wish:

Start Date -
End Date -

Goals to reach my wish/project :

1.

2.

3.

4.

5.

6.

7.

My Bucket Wish List 95.

Wish:

Start Date -
End Date -

Goals to reach my wish/project :

1.

2.

3.

4.

5.

6.

7.

My Bucket Wish List 96.

Wish:

Start Date -
End Date -

Goals to reach my wish/project :

1.

2.

3.

4.

5.

6.

7.

My Bucket Wish List 97.

Wish:

Start Date -
End Date -

Goals to reach my wish/project :

1.

2.

3.

4.

5.

6.

7.

My Bucket Wish List 98.

Wish:

Start Date -
End Date -

Goals to reach my wish/project :

1.

2.

3.

4.

5.

6.

7.

My Bucket Wish List 99.

Wish:

Start Date -
End Date -

Goals to reach my wish/project :

1.

2.

3.

4.

5.

6.

7.

My Bucket Wish List 100.

Wish:

Start Date -
End Date -

Goals to reach my wish/project :

1.

2.

3.

4.

5.

6.

7.

And Finally

I hope that you have achieved all of your dreams, whatever they were in politics.

I have enjoyed creating this book and probably will be more to come.

Peter. Churchill

Printed in Great Britain
by Amazon